Brief Encou

By

Hector Emanuelli

North Staffordshire Press

Newcastle-under-Lyme

Staffordshire

Brief Encounters

ISBN: 978-1-9998703-0-0

First published in 2013

Second Edition 2017

By

North Staffordshire Press

Brampton Business Centre

10 Queen Street

Newcastle-under-Lyme

ST5 1ED

Contents

It was a beautiful morning. Relaxing in my favourite chair, the morning sun shines brightly through the lounge window. The perfect day I say to myself for an invigorating walk, but first another cup of coffee. The lilting strain of Carol Carpenter's voice comes over the radio. The warmth of the sun, the coffee, Carol's enchanting voice all combine to send me into a deep reverie. Gone is the desire to lace up my boots and go walking! As I doze I reminisce about walks and holidays spent with my many friends over past years. I would like to share some of the fond memories with you. The following pages describe five of these holidays spent abroad with my friends, amusing incidents, adventures and some interesting brief encounters.

She was gone...but her perfume lingered on.

Sale Marasino. Sept 2001

Twelfth night has come and gone. We are now in the year of our Lord 2011- the Christmas tree decorations taken down and packed away for another year. Christmas cards perused once more. Oh, I do wish friends would improve their calligraphy! I tried and tried again, but could not decipher three of the senders. One card had no greeting at all. Never mind, whoever you were, thanks for the thought.

And so, it is time for New Year resolutions. But human frailty being what it is, it's no wonder these are inevitably soon broken. However, this year I made a firm commitment, and resolved to widen my horizons by taking more frequent and adventurous holidays. With this in mind, I studied at some length the Ramblers Association Holiday brochure looking for a suitable holiday. As I perused the brochure, for some unaccountable reason my mind slipped back some ten years to when, in October 2001, I took it upon myself to take twenty of my rambling friends to the Italian

"Lake District" in Northern Italy, where we were to spend a two-week walking holiday.

We flew from Manchester Airport and, if my memory serves me well, we landed at Verona, where a coach awaited to take us to our destination at the resort of Sale Marasino. We were met at the airport by Andrew Wood, who was to be our walking guide for the two-week holiday. We stayed at the Hotel Rotelli, which is ideally situated near the eastern shore of the Lago d'Iseo and near to the ferry terminal, which gave us frequent and reliable access to the other resorts on both shorelines of the lake.

Opposite our hotel and just a short ferry-crossing away was the island of Monte Isola, the largest lake-island in Europe. The island was free of cars and all vehicular traffic. It was to provide the location for many of our walks. Andrew proved to be a very efficient guide, and very considerate in taking into account the various capabilities of our walking group. A particularly fine walk was the climb to the summit of

Monte Isola to the Sanctuary of our Lady, where we had our picnic lunch and where we met another English walking group which, I believe, came from the Bolton area of Lancashire.

We returned to our hotel at Sale Marasino after a good day's walking to enjoy an excellent dinner, and in good time to witness the sun setting behind the Sanctuary at the top of Monte Isola. Each evening before dinner and while enjoying our pre-dinner drinks at the bar, Andrew would brief us regarding the following day's programme. On one such evening Andrew announced that we were to take the early morning ferry for Iseo after breakfast. Iseo is a small town along the southern tip of the lake. We were to start our walk for that particular day there. The town of Iseo of course gives its name to the Lago d'Iseo.

It was a hazy and misty morning as we boarded the ferry. Cloud covered the summit of Monte Isola and a slight breeze disturbing the clouds revealed for an instant the cross at the top of the sanctuary buildings.

The sun was doing its very best to break through and I felt sure it was going to be a very good day for walking. The intention was that after alighting at Iseo, Andrew would lead us through the town and into the surrounding hills, meadows and countryside, before making a loop back into Iseo for our picnic lunch.

A group of local housewives boarded the ferry with us and on this occasion the ferry did not take a direct route to Iseo, but took on further groups of ladies at the towns of Peschiera, Margolio and Sensole. It was apparent that all these groups seemed to know each other and there was great jocularity and chatter among them. I wondered why they were all heading to Iseo? I approached one of the ladies who was particularly friendly, asking:

"Come main che tutti vanno oggi ad Iseo?" - *"Why is everyone going to Iseo today?"*

"Ah signore," she said *"Oggi é giorno di mercato. Ci andiamo a fare le spese."* - "Today is market day at Iseo and we are all going shopping."

I suppose I should really have understood this as they all appeared to have purses stuffed with euro notes, and their shopping bags were empty. They all rushed off the ferry as soon as we landed at Iseo, all eager to snap up the early morning bargains. We gathered around Andrew while we deliberated on our plans for the day. It was obvious that the ladies among our group would like to participate in this and take advantage of what appeared to be a very interesting and rewarding shopping opportunity.

The sun had broken through and it looked as if it was going to be a very good day for walking. We were eager to make a start. The ladies, however, had obviously made up their minds that they would like to do a spot of shopping, and so it was decided that we should spend a little time at the market before starting our walk. It was indeed a very large market; every square, every street and every side street of the town was filled to capacity  with stalls of every description, there were multi-axled large Lorries, glass sided and refrigerated. Sun-shaded awnings protected well-displayed meats, sausages, salami and the very finest Bologna could produce. There were fish stalls, cheese from every part of Italy; leather goods and a marvellous display of household linens, curtains and laces and confectionary and bakery products to make one's mouth water. You name it; it was all there, just waiting to be snapped up. Several of the ladies that we had met on the ferry recognised us and with hand signs, in broken English and Italian, they were not slow in helping our ladies in making their purchases. Rita Dunn, for instance, bought a rather lovely and costly leather handbag. I was recently having coffee with Rita and Terry and we were talking about our past holidays. I happened to mention the day we spent at the market at Iseo.

"Yes, I do recall that day," said Rita, "and here is the very handbag I bought there. It is still as good as new!"

Eventually, Andrew managed to gather us all together and we set off on our walk with over laden rucksacks. We returned to Iseo a little later than Andrew had intended. We had all enjoyed the day immensely. As we walked back into Iseo I thought surely this is not the town we left this morning! The streets and squares were completely deserted. It was about three thirty in the afternoon, and not a soul in sight. I asked the owner of a local bar where we had stopped for a coffee.

"What has happened to the market that was here this morning?"

"Well you see," he explained, "the townspeople, shopkeepers and café owners have made an agreement with the stallholders that the town agrees to the market being held in the morning, but at three o' clock trading must cease and every stall and piece of litter be removed and we can have our town back again. As you can see," he said, "it works very well!"

That evening after dinner at the hotel there was much to talk about. The ladies from the ferry had obviously left before we had caught our ferry and no doubt would have returned with lighter purses, but bulging shopping bags. While we men had a drink or two at the bar, the ladies compared their purchases and compared the prices they had paid with those they might have paid at home.

Unfortunately, I have never kept a day-to-day journal of our many Ramblers Association holidays and have to rely solely on my now diminishing powers of recall. Certain events however will occasionally break through the mists of forgetfulness and reveal a latch that opens the door to one's memory. I can now recall with clarity one evening towards the end of our holiday in Sale Marasino, we were all gathered in the hotel lounge awaiting Andrew's briefing for the following days walking.

"Tomorrow," Andrew explained, "we shall not be walking, I have arranged for a mini coach to take us all on a sightseeing visit. We are going to Verona."

I for one was overjoyed. I have always been a great lover of all the Medieval and Renaissance towns of Northern Italy; I was so looking forward with great anticipation to the visit. Verona, the city of marble! Verona, the city of romance; Verona, where Shakespeare set his tragic love story of Romeo and Juliet: a Mecca for all lovers of Shakespeare, where today, one can attend performances in Italian in one of Verona's open-air theatres. It has always puzzled me, however, why the great Bard should have set his plays, such as *Romeo and Juliet* and *The Two Gentlemen of Verona*, in Verona. It is claimed that he never in fact set foot in Italy and that Juliet never even existed and is purely fiction. But this does not deter Shakespeare-lovers from all over the world from visiting Juliet's balcony; such is the power of the Bard of Avon's tragic story. Yes, I was really looking forward to visiting Verona, and who knows, I thought, I might even be lucky enough to meet a present-day Juliet there!

Our coach dropped us off on the outskirts of the old town. Here stands the magnificent basilica of St. Zeno. Its splendid isolation allows us to admire its striking façade, porch and bronze doors. Founded in the fifth century, its interior surpasses the exterior with fine sculptures, friezes, bronze panels, and – over the high alter – a triptych by the great master Andrea Mantegna. In my opinion, this is one of the finest churches in Verona and I would have gladly spent more time there.

Time was pressing however, and Andrew was eager to move on, there was a lot of viewing to be done as we entered the very heart of the city. There are three main piazzas in the city. Piazza dei Signori, Piazza delle Erbe (more of this later), and the main square, Piazza Bra. Why it should bear this particular nomenclature baffles me, after all there is no sponsorship boutique selling such apparel in the Piazza. As far as I can tell the name goes back to the medieval times, before it came into modern-day use. We did a lot of viewing during the morning, jostling our way through the busy streets whilst always keeping Andrew within our sights, so many churches, palaces, monuments, the town Hall at Piazza Bra, the Scaligeri Palace and tombs. The Scaligeri family produced the Lords of Verona during the medieval period until the city came under the protection of the Venetian Republic. I do recall seeing a statue of the Lion of Saint Marc in one of the square. However, I cannot at this stage remember which one. Verona prospered under the protection of Venice in the Renaissance period.

The main attraction in the Piazza Bra, is of course, the Roman amphitheatre, the most perfectly preserved of all such Roman amphitheatres, second only in size to the Coliseum in Rome. It has a seating capacity of 2,220 and is regularly used today for the production of operas. Tom Waterhouse and I entered the amphitheatre; the Veronese call it the Arena. We climbed to the very top and sat on the cold marble seats and gazed down into the pit where technicians were busily engaged in erecting scaffolding and canvas scenery.

"Do you think they are preparing for the production of Verdi's Aida?" I asked Tom.

"You might well be right," he said.

In my mind's eye, I pictured the scene towards the end of the opera with the great triumphal march as the wild beasts from Africa with the attendant Egyptian lance bearers march in what seems a never-ending procession across the stage to Verdi's orchestral crescendo, the music filling the arena and spilling into the Piazza Bra, where dining tourists enjoying their meal would wish that they were at the performance.

"We could have been there tonight," says the husband to his wife, "if you had not spent our last precious Euros on that expensive handbag.'

My reverie was suddenly shattered by Tom saying to me:

"Come along Hector, Andrew is waiting for us below."

Andrew explained that we were all rather leg weary after the morning's jostling through the crowded streets and that we should take a break/do our own thing/rest a while, with perhaps a cappuccino, and we should meet up again in an hour's time at Juliet's house to resume our perambulation of the city. Most of the ladies made for the shops. I thought to myself this would be the perfect opportunity to escape for a while from all the culture and art treasuries that were giving us mental indigestion. I would venture behind the streets and discover what went on in present-day

Verona, away from the tourists and the elegant restaurants and bars. Within a brisk ten-minute walk, and after crossing Via Mazzini, I found myself in the side and back streets of the city. Somewhere to eat, I thought: to savour the local cuisine and atmosphere. I came across a trattoria with parasol-shaded tables; every table occupied not by staid and serious tourists but by a jolly laughing crowd of what appeared to be people taking their normal lunch break. The atmosphere was bohemian, as though I had strayed in the café act of Puccini's La Bohème. But this was no Parisian scene: this was purely a group of Italians enjoying themselves. I ventured into the shady interior. This was also crowded, but I managed to spot a vacant table in the far corner of the room. I made my way there, sat down and within seconds the waiter was there to take my order. I plumped for a plate of ravioli con sugp di pomodori e funghi with Parmigiano and a glass of lambrusco wine to complete my enjoyment. It seemed, however, that I was not to have the privilege of eating alone. She seemed to appear from nowhere.

"Permesso" she said, indicating the empty seat at my rather cramped table. A polite way of saying, "may I join you?"

"Certainly," I said as I re-arranged the condiments, giving her more space.

She must have ordered her meal in advance because the waiter immediately placed her order before her, an enticing plate of insalata primavera with prosciutto and half a bottle of Pellegrino sparkling water. She must be a regular customer, I thought, and this would most likely be her favourite table. She was very elegant, wearing an obviously tailored suit with white blouse, she wore no jewellery, and I got the distinct impression that she was either a business executive or perhaps even a model. We ate for a while in silence until I broke the ice and said to her:

"the food here is very good."

"Yes," she replied, "I eat here every day during my lunch break; my office is just around the corner." This comment confirmed my suspicion that she was an executive of some kind. We made polite conversation for a while. I explained that I was with a group of friends 'doing the city.' I explained that we were to meet in a short while at Juliet's house. She gave me an engaging smile as she said:

"Oh signor, do please be careful there, it is the favourite haunt of pickpockets you know." I thanked her kindly for this advice. By way of continuing our conversation, I said to her:

"You are indeed very fortunate living and working in such a fine city."

"Well actually," she said, "although my work is here in Verona I live in Vicenza, which, as you may know, is between Verona and Venice."

"You are indeed doubly blessed to be living among those Palladian villas," I replied, adding "you may

16

know that many of our English country homes, town halls and civic buildings, yes even the Capitol in Washington owe much to the influential designs of their architect, Andrea Palladio."

"You are quite right of course," she said. "As a matter of fact, I live quite close to Villa Rotonda, which as you may know is one of his masterpieces." A quick glance at her wristwatch signalled the end of our conversation. "*Sono in ritardo,* (I am late)" she said. She got up from the table and extending her hand she added "*E stato un vero piacere* (it has been a great pleasure)!" And without further ado she was gone. Yes, she was elegant and very charming, but for some reason she did not come up to my expectations of a modern-day Juliet! A quick cup of coffee and I was on my way to meet my fellow ramblers at Juliet's house. The lady from Vicenza had of course given me direction, adding that one had only to mention the name Juliet and I could not go wrong.

"In any case," she said, "just follow the Japanese: we all know how the Japanese love Shakespeare."

The approach to Juliet's house is via a narrow passageway, the walls of which are completely covered in graffiti in the form of lover's signatures, entwined hearts and declarations of eternal love. Some of the graffiti is quite small, some large. The whole gives a rather attractive modern art appearance and would not look out of place in the Tate Modern. Most of my friends, including nine of our ladies, were already gathered in the courtyard below the balcony, together with many other tourists of various nationalities. Each of the ladies would take it in turns to enter the house and appear for a brief instant on the balcony to be photographed. Even our veteran 80 year-old Margaret Cox and "little" Mary Green took their turn. This of course all took time and as the gentlemen's arms were raised holding aloft their cameras so were their jackets, revealing hip pockets, with in many cases bulging wallets in full view.

Immediately, the warning of my lady in Vicenza sprang to view. 'Pick pockets!' I felt a hand on my hip! It was mine, instinctively carried there by the sight of all those easy pickings for the pickpockets.

When the photographic session was over we left Juliet's balcony, and little did I realise it at the time, but within half an hour I was to discover, meet and even speak for a short time to what was my vision of a modern-day Veronese Juliet! "Little" Mary Green and myself were walking together after having left the balcony, where ladies were still awaiting their turn to be photographed as aspiring Juliet's. We call her "little" because like me, she is short of stature. She does not mind this of course because she knows that we love her!

But Mary and I had no time for coffee. We were intent on exploring further. A few minutes later we stumbled upon another of the many colourful Piazzas of Verona, the Piazza delle Erbe. It was there right in the middle of the Piazza that my vision of the ideal modern-day

Veronese Juliet arrested my attention. Theatrical casting directors the world over will seek out their ideal Juliet, she would have to be tall, slender, blue eyed with long flowing blond hair. My Juliet was not at all like that. She was not tall but of medium height, slim-waisted, wearing a knee length skirt revealing her shapely legs, white shirt and gloves, her chestnut coloured hair was topped with a cute little coquettish policewoman's hat. Yes, you have guessed. It was a policewoman. Had I overacted you will ask, no it was not the uniform that had arrested my attention, but the way in which she controlled the traffic with complete authority, the graceful movements of white-gloved hands and outstretched arms, her balletic movements and the way her head and shoulders turned, stretching her white shirt, enhancing the curves of her breasts. I was won over!

"Lend me your guide book Mary, I won't be long." Playing the role of a lost tourist with my guide book in hand and with some trepidation, I approached her.

"Excuse me officer," I said, "could you please tell me what the name of this piazza is?" That was as good an opening line as I could think of on the spur of the moment.

"*Si signor,*" she replied. "This is the Piazza delle Erbe, many of our Italian cities have piazzas so named, and it is where the weekly produce markets are held." Pausing for a moment whilst she dealt with two impatient and noise Vespa riders she added. "*Deve ritornare domain* (you should come back tomorrow) *domain è giorno di mercato* (tomorrow is market day)!" Then with a lowered voice and a conspiratorial smile she added, as if she was talking and confirmed to herself, "*E domain sarò libera* (and tomorrow I am off duty)!" I wondered for a brief instant whether that was a very discreet invitation, but quickly realised this was purely wishful thinking on my part. Traffic was beginning to build up. I was obviously interfering with her duties. With a most apologetic smile she said to me:

"You must ignore me signor, otherwise I shall arrest you for loitering with intent."

She said this while tapping with her white-gloved hand the highly polished and chic little holster that hugged her hip. I mumbled some form of apologetic excuse and made my way to the kerbside where Mary was still waiting for me. I wondered, did that holster really contain a tiny and bejewelled Beretta or was it her Gucci vanity bag? Little Mary remonstrated with me:

"Come on Hector," she said. "The others have all gone ahead, we shall lose them."

"Don't worry," I said. "We shall soon catch them up."

"What was that all about?" asked Mary.

"I'll tell you later, Mary" I said as I kept glancing back from time to time.

Yes, she was still there performing with her ballet movements as she controlled the traffic as if conducting an orchestra! We soon caught up with the others; apparently, we had not been missed. We gathered at the fourteenth century fortress of Castelvecchio. Strong bastions supported crenulated walls and towers topped by merlons, the shape of which depended on which ruling faction was in power at the time, rectangular for the Guelphs and swallow - tailed for the Ghibellines. Inside the palace is the City Museum with its collection of statuary paintings by the great masters, jewellery and weaponry.

From the fortress, we made our way along the shore of the Adige, which meanders in a graceful curve of the Grand Canal in Venice. We took a welcome break, standing on the bridge enjoying the view back towards the city with Lamberti tower, the tallest building in Verona, showing off the pretty octagonal top of the tower. Vistas of ivory and cream painted villas, the rosy-red facades of Verona and the terracotta roofs, make a wonderful picture with the tall green black cypress trees punctuating the scene like challenging exclamation marks which seem to say 'Look well upon the scene all of you that pass this way! You will see no better view in all of Europe!' I wondered what Canaletto would have made of it.

Our day in Verona was unfortunately drawing to its close. It was a great pity but we did not have time to visit the famous Giusti Gardens with their woodland paths overlooking the floral displays, the foundations, the hedge maze and the spiral staircase which leads to the belvedere with its splendid views overlooking the city. Our coach was waiting to take us back to our Hotel Rotelli at Sale Marasino. We all relaxed on the homeward journey and I had an opportunity to explain to Mary Green my brief encounter with "Juliet" in the Piazza delle Erbe! We all had a lot to talk about at dinner that evening, and as the sun went down behind the sanctuary on Monte Isola I thought: 'Yes, it would indeed have been a treat to have been able to attend market day in Piazza delle Erbe tomorrow!'

During the last few days of our two-week holiday we had been deliberating between ourselves as to what would have been an appropriate gift that we could present to Andrew, in recognition of the friendliness and expert guidance that he had shown us during our many walks. During my many chats with Andrew I realised that he was a lover of classical music, and so it was that on reaching the end of one of our walks and when his back was turned we purchased three CDs which we felt would please him. These we presented to him on our last evening. He was extremely pleased, and I know he liked them, because when we all returned home I received a letter from his wife saying how much he had appreciated the gesture and that we had made a good choice!

That was over ten years ago, and now back at home in Stoke-on-Trent, I walk the wet and familiar streets of the Potteries. I take long and solitary country walks, although now with advancing years and being visually impaired, one or two of my friends - no doubt well -

intentioned and with my welfare at heart - have suggested that I begin to take things easy. They say "Hector, why do you not join the group of local seniors who walk the tow paths and stroll the local paths?" Their thoughts are meant well, but as long as I have the semblance of a "tiger in the tank" I much prefer to continue with my long walks. I am a great believer in solitary walking as it helps clear my mind from imagined slights and the petty problems and worries of daily life. As I battle the winds and driving rain along my favourite walk along the Mam Tor Ridge, my mind clears to a virgin white canvas, my imaginary paintbrush dips into the palette of forgotten memories which bursts through the clouds of forgetfulness and soon covers the canvas with colourful incidents and pictures of walks and holidays during the past years. Those weeks spent in the Brecon Beacons, the Yorkshire Dales, the Lake District, when it rained for a whole week, but we still had such good fun. The Scotland fortnight where I scrambled among the heather for my lost dentures! My Olympic climb to the high peak in the Austrian Alps, from where I gazed down across the border into Italy. The scrumptious vanilla ice cream served with apple strudel in that little café in Ortisei in the Italian Dolomites. I have never tasted ice cream so good and I know a thing or two about ice cream! All these thoughts come to me like shafts of illumination, they crystallize and form gems of happy memories spent on my walking holidays at home and abroad. My worries forgotten, my blank canvas is soon filled and I make my way home invigorated and ready for the next task. I reach my front door, I step over the accumulation of junk mail, careful not to slip on the glossy magazines, and I make my way into the kitchen. A pile of washing up awaits me from the morning's breakfast. "I must get another bottle of washing-up liquid," I say to myself.

BOARIO
TERME
COSTA
VOLPINO
BOSSICO
LOVERE
CASTRO
PISOGNE
RANZANICO
ENDINE
SOLTO COLLINA
BIANZANO
VALMAGGIORE
RIVA
DI SOLTO
SPINONE
AL LAGO
S. FELICE
AL LAGO
CORNA
TRENTAPASSI
GAVERINA
TERME
MONASTEROLO
DEL CASTELLO
L. D'ENDINE
L A G O
VELLO
CASAZZA
FONTENO
ZONE
PARZANICA
D'ISEO
MARONE
I. DI LORETO
VIGOLO
SALE
MARASINO
ADRARA
S. ROCCO
MONTE
ISOLA
TAVERNOLA
BERGAMASCA
VIADANICA
I. DI S. PAOLO
SULZANO
PREDORE
VILLONGO
SARNICO
PILZONE
PARATICO
CLUSANE
ISEO
F R A N C I A C O R T A
CAPRIOLO
CORTEFRANCA
TORBIERE
D'ISEO
PROVAGLIO D'ISEO
ADRO
MONTICELLI
BRUSATI
OME
ERBUSCO
PASSIRANO
RODENGO SAIANO
CAZZAGO
BORNATO

AMSTERDAM
BERLINO
PARIGI
VIENNA

| Golf | Bicycle riding | Fishing | Thermal | Castle | Horse riding | Sailing |

28

Austria 2002

Manchester airport early one August morning, the 31st to be exact, bleary eyes and very tired we assemble in twos and threes until we are all gathered together, all twenty of us, members of the Stoke on Trent and Newcastle ramblers, ready for two weeks walking in the Austrian Alps. After many cups of coffee and the odd consoling brandy we hear the long-awaited call, 'Passengers for flight F3771 to Zurich please assemble at gate 27.'

We arrive at Zurich airport on time having been dined and wined by Swiss Air and were now relaxed. Having collected our luggage we were met at arrivals by Keith, who was to be our walk leader for the two weeks that we were to spend at the Upper Inn valley of Austria. He was bronzed, sturdy and looking extremely fit. Introductions all round, and then I said to Terry Dunn, who happened to be standing next to me:

"My word Terry, Keith looks very fit, I wonder what he has in store for us?"

With Keith now in charge we boarded our private coach which was to drive us along the Upper Inn Valley to our destination in the winter ski resorts of Ladis, Fiss and Serhaus, which would be the bases for our walking holiday. We then had a wonderful drive through many pretty alpine villages, the houses decked with colourful window boxes, all with cascading crimson geraniums. Our hotel was the Hotel Goies at Ladis where we were met by our hostess Barbara and her caring daughter Nicole. I must have been the first off the coach as she came towards me:

"Welcome to the Hotel Goies," she said, "my name is Barbara and this is my daughter Nicole."

Nicole said, "Welcome Herr Emanuelli, this is your key to room 27." In true Tyrolean fashion there were hugs and kisses all round as we made our way to our respective rooms. This welcome augrs, well I thought to myself, I'm sure I shall enjoy my stay here!

Barbara waters her Geraniums

The Goies, although a small family run hotel does not lack any of the winter resort facilities. There was a heated boot and changing room, which proved ideal when returning from our mountain walks, and there were ski racks for use by the winter sports enthusiasts, a Jacuzzi and gym, and I was even able to have a neck and shoulder massage by a visiting Swedish masseuse. The bedrooms were warm and comfortable and the dining room and lounges gave out that true Tyrolean atmosphere.

During the two weeks that we were to spend at Ladis we got to know the village quite well, as well as the neighbouring resorts of Fiss and Serhaus. There was a village shop at Ladis which we patronised for the purchase of our picnic snacks for our days walking. It was there I bought my favourite Ritter chocolate and drinking water. The shop assistant, who for want of a better name we called Helga, was in fact very grumpy. Making up our ham and cheese rolls she would slap on the slices of ham or cheese with total disregard for any finesse in the operation. Alan Crisp didn't get on very well with her at all and claimed that she had attended charm school, failed her tests and had not had her fees reimbursed.

The village pub however was another story altogether. Situated only a short distance from the hotel, it was small and strictly alpine in character. We would meet there after dinner several times a week. The innkeeper was very friendly and entertained us as we mixed with the locals. He spoke English well, was well travelled, and most evenings he would entertain us by demonstrating his fire eating act. He would tell lurid tales of his travels abroad and had a collection of various kinds of hats which he displayed behind the bar. One such hat was an English policeman's helmet. Each in turn we were obliged to try this on to everyone's merriment, especially the locals. Of course, we would drink the local brews, and I took the opportunity of introducing to my friends my favourite tipples of sambuca, amaretto and Frangelico. We got quite merry during the course of the evening, until I think it was Phil who called out:

"Now come along you lot, it's getting late, time to get back to the Hotel!" We made our way slowly back to the hotel, it was a gloriously warm, dark night and the stars were bright in the sky.

The innkeepers name was Heimo and during the course of the week as we entered the pub he would call out to his regular customers "Achtung, Achtung, put away your guns; Hector's gang is here again!" Of course, we did not visit the pub every night but we made full use of the other attractions of the hotel, the Solarium, the Jacuzzi and saunas. Some nights Mavis would arrange a quiz night and then Barbara would organise a bingo session. I am not a lover of bingo myself but I never missed the chance of attending the bingo night, it was such a pleasure to listen to Barbara calling out the numbers in English with her lovely Austrian accent. As we made our way to the hotel those fateful words from the last act of Puccini's Tosca came to my mind "E lucevano le stelle." Yes, the stars were certainly shining brightly that September evening.

After a day's energetic walking it was always with anticipation that we looked forward to our evening dinner, having shed our boots and rucksacks, showered and changed, we would gather in the cosiness of the dining room. The food was always excellent and elegantly served by Barbara's two daughters, Nicole and Sonia, who were always beautifully dressed in their beautiful Austrian gowns, with a different style each evening! One evening, Nicole, bending over the table to serve me my soup, revealed, but very demurely the merest glimpse of a bare shoulder, my admiring glance was rewarded by a delightful smile. Yvonne who was sitting opposite me at the table exclaimed:

Nicole and Sonia

"Eat your soup Hector! You know you are much too old for that!" I was quickly brought back to earth. The dinners were always jolly affairs, exchanges of confidences, secrets revealed, many after dinner jokes and even Sheila and Joan, who were normally very quiet, could tell a joke or two.

You will be wondering about our walking experiences and what sort of a guy our walk leader was. It would be difficult to recall each walking day in particular, however there are three walks that stand out in my memory and I will relate these later. As it was to be expected, the walks were hard and often quite tough, we suffered, but there was always the recompense of glorious views. Paths were often stony with jagged rocks, huge boulders, and dizzy heights with windswept peaks and forest paths that often had dangerous protruding roots that required one's complete attention. There were icy paths with sheer drops, however, all these hazards we grew to take in our stride. After all this is why we had come on a walking alpine holiday. We were of course in the safe hands of Keith our leader who was a professional, patient and caring leader. His knowledge of the local flora and fauna was unique, and as we walked along he would point out the late flowering gentian crocus and where the early spring flowers, now of course sadly gone, would appear. He would point out the cry and flight of the nutcracker, buzzards, black squirrels and a tiny baby shrew that once crossed our path. Keith explained to us all about the local customs, and he knew all the best hostelries. Keith's rucksack weighed a ton and I know because I tried it on! Keith as a trek leader was prepared for any possible eventuality, he carried survival and first aid kits, spare walking poles, water, socks, hats, gloves, jacket, maps, compass, and it was said he even carried spare boots size six, for the ladies of course. We were indeed in very good hands with Keith as our leader.

The Via Claudia Walk

It was Saturday the 6th of September and it was also my 82nd birthday. Keith had decided to take us on what is known as the Via Claudia walk. This walk is 13k long with some 450m of climbing and contours the countryside and mountain hamlets of Serfaus, Dranus, Reis and Prutz. At times there were dizzy heights, dangerous paths windswept vistas of distant peaks. We occasionally came across sheltered aspects with alpine meadows full of grazing cows, cream and chocolate coloured, each wearing its own tinkling bell.

The River Inn

We took advantage of these spots to enjoy our picnic lunches whilst inquisitive mountain goats would nuzzle into our rucksacks hoping to find an appetising snack! From the windswept heights we would look down the pine clad slopes to the far distant valley bottoms. We could see tiny white painted houses and farmsteads like some confetti scattered after some wedding feast. With ever decreasing paths we reached the valley bottom and emerged onto the Via Claudia. This is the road that the Roman legions once trod. We follow the river Inn which comes rushing down from the Kaunertal Glacier, making its way to the city of Innsbruck. The water blue green in colour splashes and foams as it breaks through protruding rocks and for some reason it reminds me of a frothy peppermint milkshake. Several of us take off our boots and socks and bathe our aching feet in the waters, not for long however, the water was simply ice cold. Following the river through the pleasant country paths we enter the town of Prutz.

Here we feast ourselves on coffees, ice creams, apple strudel and sachertorte. This was a very enjoyable finish to my 82nd birthday walk! Back at the hotel Keith informed us that tomorrow would be a "free" day; we would not be doing any walking. Several of our group decided to take a trip to Innsbruck. Others just relaxed with their book, but I had decided to explore the village with Barbara Foster, and in the afternoon we played table tennis in the relaxed atmosphere of the Hotel garden.

After an early dinner we all assembled to board our coach which was to take us to our Tyrolean Night, a large mountain ski resort hotel at Serfhaus.

Tyrolean Night

The Hotel was quite full when we arrived; Keith had reserved some tables for us, near the bar and quite close to the stage. He had saved a seat for me, very close to the stage. I wondered about this at the time but I soon found out later in the evening! Drinks were served all-round, then the lights were dimmed and the fun began. The band struck up, violins, horns, flute and accordions, on came the dancing girls, all in Tyrolean costumes. A huge maypole was erected on stage, with their gaily coloured ribbons. They gyrated in ever changing formation around the pole and then reversed the process to much applause. A maypole in Austria, I thought it was a purely English custom!

Then on came the Tyrolean men with thighs like tree trunks, big bottoms, leather shorts, the women too, big bosomed with swirling skirts and much thigh slapping, yodelling, dancing and gyrating all to very energetic music. Then a huge wooden log was brought on stage. Two burly Tyrolean woodsmen armed with huge axes began the rhythmic chopping of the log. Wood splinters covered most of the stage and the audience too. On came the Tyrolean maids with pans, and brushed and swept the place clean to much merriment and applause. Then came the dancer girls, younger, prettier and inviting, now I know why Keith had saved

41

me the seat! The dancing was in full swing, she left the stage and came straight to my seat and yanked me onto the stage.

"You will dance with me?" She enquired.

"But I don't dance," I explained.

"Not to worry mine Herr," she said. "Just rest your head on my bosom and leave the rest to me." This was an offer I could not refuse. She yanked me onto the stage and whirled me around the floor as if I was a rag doll. I was giddy, excited and exhilarated. Then the dance was over and she returned me to my seat.

"You will perhaps come again", she said.

"Now we have met how can I refuse." The night proceeded in similar fashion, but after many drinks and much laughter it was time to leave what had been a most memorable evening, and so back to the tranquillity of our hotel. On reflection, back at the hotel

I realised why Keith had reserved that seat for me so close to the stage!

The Anton Renk Walk

The morning after our Tyrolean night frolic, Keith announced that we were to attempt the Anton Renk Hut Walk. It was a glorious morning when we set off on this 14k walk, with a 550m climb. During our stay at Ladis we have become accustomed to the various hazards of Alpine walking, dizzy heights, forest paths with slippery protruding roots, icy slopes with alarming drops, breath taking climbs and all these hazards we had learnt to take in our stride. Around mid-day we came across a rather pleasant grassy knoll and it was here we decided to take our lunch time stop. After lunch most of the group decided that they would continue their walk by contouring the lower slopes and return to the knoll where they would meet up with the six of us who were going to climb up to the Anton Renk Hut, higher up the mountain. The hut is provided by the Austrian Alpine club as a refuge for lost climbers. After what was a pleasant climb we reached the hut, which was splendidly isolated, built of forest timber and very solid. All six of us filled the cosy interior where we drank our coffee and I ate one of my chocolate Ritter bars. A passing Austrian walker approached us and very kindly took our group photograph. I have never seen a copy, but no doubt it will have been seen in some Austrian walking magazine.

Mary Green relaxes

After a very pleasant descent from the Anton Renk refuge hut we soon met up with the rest of our group who were waiting for us at the appointed spot. Wally, we were told had lost his spectacles. Despite careful searches around the picnic area they were nowhere to be found. Several of us retraced Wally's steps among the boulders and stony paths and some time was spent searching but all to no avail. It was not until sometime later in the day that they came to light! Securely tucked away at the very bottom of his rucksack! I will not mention what Margaret his wife said to Wally, remembering at the same time that earlier that week he had left his rucksack on one of the coaches that we used! The rucksack was returned to him some three days later. Back at the hotel we had a lot to talk about after dinner, Wally was forgiven and we had all had a very enjoyable day.

Then Keith spoke up and reminded us that tomorrow would be our last day.

"Tomorrow", he said "You are going to have a day that you will remember for a very long time to come." How right he was! "Tomorrow," he said, "we are going by coach to visit the Kaunertal Glacier, high in the Austrian Alps!"

Our Last day: The Kaunertal Glacier

The romantic Kauner Valley runs right into the world

Kaunertal

of Lake Weissee and the Gepatsch Glacier where the breathtaking beauty of the Austrian Alps is revealed in all its glory. Leaving Prutz we branch off into the Kauner Valley, high above the road. In the forest is the Castle Bernago which was once the hunting lodge of the Emperor Maximillian and close by is also the Pilgrimage church Kaltenbrun, a rare treasure and much visited. On our journey, we pass the Kauner Valley Folk museum, although we do not have time to stop. We reach Fechten, the capital of the Kauner Valley with its many sporting facilities, indoor swimming pool, tennis courts, bowling alley, saunas and solariums, and many other enticing facilities.

We drive on however along the aptly named Panorama Road which is 27k long and passes through some of the most breathtaking scenery. We pass the biggest reservoir in Western Austria and the 7k long Gepatsch Reservoir where a 14k pressure tunnel feeds the Power Station at Prutz. We come to Gepatsch where the cows come down from the higher slopes for their summer holidays and continue past the Nature Trail through ancient larch forests, mountain streams and lakes. We have magnificent views all around us.

Our coach now leaves the Valley floor and climbs steadily with many hair pin bends to the Mountain Restaurant at 2750ft above sea level and then we have before us the eternal ice of the Kaunertal Glacier, glistening in the afternoon sun. We relax on the sun terrace as we watch distance skiers gliding down the slopes and marvel at this amazing ice world.

I sit there drinking my delicious hot chocolate and mulled wine; I am accompanied by Barbara Foster, Marty Green and nearby sits Arthur Rushton, the perfect English gentleman with his customary pot of tea! Suddenly our reverie is broken as Keith calls out:

"Come along folks we have a lot more to do and see." We are directed towards the cable car which is to take us further up the mountain. We climb aboard, the air is becoming much colder now with icy blasts to the viewing platform, where we loiter awhile enjoying the distant views.

We vaguely assume that we can now descend and return to the restaurant. Not so!

"Those of you that would like to go a little higher follow me," says Keith. I am one of the few that volunteers. We take the chair lift that seems to dangle perilously in thin air, our knuckles hang on the hand hold, our legs dangle in space and then suddenly we touch the sheer wall of the mountain face, frightening but very exhilarating. I am now feeling very cold and my breath comes in short gasps.

The chair-lift eventually drops us off, but there facing us is a most awesome sight, a very narrow ridge path rising steeply to the summit. We start off slowly, and then as the lack of oxygen takes its toll, we slow our pace until we proceed a few feet at a time, constantly stopping to regain one's breath. I feel that I can go no further, should I be doing this at my age I say to myself. But I am determined. I must go on. I am virtually on my hands and knees as I make the last few feet. Suddenly a hand shoots out from behind the rock, I grasp it.

"Well done Hector," says Keith, "you have just reached the summit. Take a rest and have a celebratory drink." With my ice cold fingers I manage to unscrew my flask and take a drink, and then another as I slowly recover.

Still short of breath with misty eyes I gazed into the distance.

"Down there," said Keith "is Italy."

"Thank you, Keith," I said "you have made me a very happy man!"

Now all re-united back at the Restaurant, we all enjoyed a few celebratory drinks and all agreed that Keith had kept his word when he promised us a day that we would never forget!

Auf Wiedersehen.

Two weeks have so quickly flown by. We have had a simply wonderful time, a truly memorable Austrian Holiday. We say farewell to Keith with our very grateful thanks for leading us on such amazing walks! We hug and kiss Barbara for her wonderful hospitality and not forgetting a goodbye kiss to sweet Nicole! We reluctantly board our coach to Zurich Airport, to Manchester and home to Stoke-on-Trent.

Tuscany 2004

The postman was early that morning. It came through the letter box and landed on my doormat with a thump! The 'Ramblers' Holiday Brochure. A quick glance through its pages brought me to the Italian section, there it was - 'Tuscany Life Style.' Eight days of walking and cooking in Tuscany. This appealed to me immediately and it seemed that Neil Oakden of the Biddulph Ramblers had also spotted this and within a few days had contacted me to see whether I was interested. I was of course, and within a very short time Neil had enrolled some sixteen members from the Biddulph, Stoke and Newcastle Group and the holiday was booked.

We left Manchester on the 26th of September 2004 for Bologna airport. A short but pleasant drive through the Tuscan countryside brought us to our destination at the Hotel Giardini in San Marcello. Our hosts Cinzia and her husband Rudy met us with welcoming drinks, and then Rudy helped us with our luggage to our rooms. After we had settled in, Cinzia introduced herself.

"My name is Cinzia. I am not a professional cook and I have never been to a professional cooking school. I was born in a family where good home cooking was considered to be important. In fact, my mother and my grandmother taught me all the recipes which we are going to cook together. I am not a teacher, and my kitchen is not a class room. I hope you will enjoy cooking with me, and then when you leave at the end of your holiday you will take a bit of Tuscany with you, and you will remember Cinzia and Rudy with pleasure."

Jock, who was to be our walks leader, then introduced himself and explained the programme; immediately after breakfast Rudy was to take us in his bus to the start of the day's walk, and then pick us up at the end of the walk to return us to the hotel in time to start work in the kitchen. On days when longer walks were envisaged Rudy would return us in good time for dinner and we would not have to do any cooking. Finally, one day of our holiday would be devoted to a visit to the City of Florence.

Cooking with Cinzia

Our cooking afternoons with Cinzia were always very relaxed and informal. Unlike the chefs we see on television there was never any swearing or culinary disasters. Cinzia would split us up in to teams of two. One team would wash and prepare the vegetables whilst other teams would prepare the meats, including wild boar and jugged rabbit. Others would make fresh pasta using six eggs and a kilo of flour; this would then be rolled out either for making spaghetti or talgliatelle or ravioli and so on. Parsley, garlic and cheese had to be chopped to make the filling for the ravioli. We also dipped courgette flowers in batter and deep fried them which made a delicious snack, which we ate while going about our other tasks.

Ray Lovatt thought it would be a good idea to reverse the procedure and teach Cinzia how to make some good old English chips. He made a godly quantity together with some fritters. We enjoyed this treat. Cinzia and Rude had their fair share too, and enjoyed them immensely.

After our cooking sessions we usually changed and took a pre-dinner stroll through the town, getting to know the shops and the locals. They were always pleased to see us and wanting to know where we were going on our walks. In order to keep up my reputation, I usually sought out the most attractive ladies and engaged them in conversation. My excuse, of course, was that I was practicing my Italian. Well, what better excuse could one give! It was also true, but I must admit I did enjoy it too!

Walking in Tuscany

Mountains, valleys, alpine meadows and remote villages all featured in our walking programme from the Hotel Giardini. Jock, our intrepid, agile and fit leader was - as his name implies - a Scotsman. He was a veteran of some sixty plus years, bearded, very capable and considerate, with regard to the less fit of our group. Jock had only one fault, his Scottish accent was a great impediment and very often we did not understand him. Pointing to a distant peak or remote village he would utter something in explanation, but often we could not understand whether he was referring to Mow Cop or Scholar Green!

Two walks in particular are worth mentioning, 'The Two Bridges Walk,' and the 'Monte Rondinaio Walk', one ancient, the other modern.

The Two Bridges

Walking along the valley of the river Lima we made a pleasant stop in sight of our first bridge, a huge arched 13th century stone construction spanning the River Lima. We rested here among the boulder-strewn banks where we had our picnic lunch and bathed our feet in the chilly water. Crossing the bridge we took the steeply rising stone-paved path with drifts of wild cyclamen on either side.

The bridge over the river Lima...

Still climbing we reached the remote village of Piglio, where we discovered what appeared to be the only cafe in the village. The cafe was very busy with the local villagers, but they very kindly made way for us, here we refreshed ourselves with iced tea, ice creams, cappuccino etc. I spoke to several of the locals; they wanted to know where we were heading. I explained that we were to cross the Lima a little further on by the new bridge. They gave me a knowing smile and wished us a pleasant walk! I guessed they knew very well what we were in for, giving Jock a knowing wink!

We climbed a little further, and there it was, Jock's 'Modern Bridge.' This was reportedly the world's longest pedestrian suspension bridge. It was a steel construction crossing of what I can only describe as a junior version of the Grand Canyon and it was frankly terrifying. The steel decking of the bridge's floor also allowed one to peer down into the depths of the ravine. We crossed in single file, and as we reached the middle the bridge swayed perilously, and we held on for our dear lives as we climbed the far bank. We were a bag of nerves as we gathered on the far bank of the ravine. Jock smiled wryly, but we eventually forgave him and thanked him for giving us the thrill of a lifetime. I'm sure that those villagers at Piglio knew what we were in for when we told them we were going to cross the Lima by the modern bridge. But they never let on!

...and the new one!

Monte Rondinaio

We were all looking forward to climbing the Monte Rondinaio. Rudy had dropped us off and we walked to the village of Abetone where we took the ski-lift, which took us further up the mountain. We became enveloped in a dense mountain mist, which slowed our progress considerably. Jock warned us that on no account must we lose sight of the person in front, and paths were sometimes quite hazardous as we made our way to the summit. At 6,000 feet, we reached the alpine refuge hut and the welcome comfort of a hot stove where we were able to dry out. In no time at all, hot soup was provided and delicious plates of pasta and, of course, the obligatory glasses of Chianti.

We met there several Italian ramblers and I soon engaged them in conversation. I asked them if they had ever walked part of the Via Francigina. They said they had not, but had come across the way-marked signs in white and red with the figure of pilgrim. The Via Francigina, I explained, is a pilgrim route and is 1,600 kilometres long. It was in the year 990 that Archbishop Sigeric of Canterbury first made his pilgrimage to Rome and the Holy Lands, setting off from Canterbury and crossing through France, Switzerland, over the Italian Alps through Piedmont and Lombardy, through my home district of Bardi, into Tuscany and then onto Rome. In 1994 the Via Francigina was declared a 'Cultural itinerary of the Council of Europe,' and is sponsored by the World Tourist Organisation and the Vatican City.

Jock explained that the path we had taken to reach the refuge hut was the path taken by Hannibal when he

had passed this way with his elephants, with the conquest of Rome in his thoughts. This was the same path, I explained to Jock that passes through my parents' home town of Bardi. Local legend has it that Hannibal left the last of his 37 elephants there as he retreated before the victorious Romans. The elephant was named Bardus and the children of the village adopted it as their pet, tending and feeding it until it died some years later on the banks of the river Ceno, at the foot of the rock on which the Castello di Bardi was to be built eight hundred years later! With Jock's expert guidance, we reached the base and were very relieved to see Rudy waiting there for us. It had been a truly exciting and exhilarating day on Monte Rondinaio.

Zuccotto

Zuccotto is an Italian dessert which is served at parties or on festive occasions. I have made this dessert several times at home. One afternoon in the Giardini kitchen I was busily engaged in chopping parsley and garlic. Cinzia happened to be standing nearby and I absent-mindedly said to her:

"Cinzia, avete mai preparato uno zuccotto per i vostri ospiti?" (Cinzia have you ever made a zuccotto for your guests?)

"Not very often," she replied. "I know the dish of course, but if you would like to make it for our gala dinner dessert I'll get the ingredients tomorrow when I go shopping." Panic now set in. What had I let myself in for? It is one thing preparing this in the comfort of one's own kitchen, but in a strange kitchen with unfamiliar utensils this was asking for trouble. But I had now committed myself, so I gave the list of ingredients to Cinzia. This included whipping cream, icing sugar, roasted hazelnuts, dark chocolate, cocoa powder, fresh cherries, chocolate sponge cake, brandy and Cointreau liquor. True to her word, Cinzia had produced all the ingredients and they were waiting for me in the kitchen. I enlisted the help of my friend Pam Lovatt and together we set to work. We whipped the cream and folded in the hazelnuts, grated chocolate, stoned and halved the cherries, added sugar and left the mixture to chill in the fridge. We now had to slice the chocolate sponge and line two glass pudding basins with sponge, soaking it with the brandy and Cointreau mixture. Cinzia had brought a full bottle of each and it came in very handy for the occasional slurp or two while we were cooking. We finally filled the basins with the cream mixture and Cinzia suggested we should put them in the fridge. "They will make an excellent dessert for out Gala dinner!" Pam and I crossed our fingers!

Our Day in Florence

At last our eagerly awaited day in Florence had arrived. I love Florence and over the years I have visited it several times. The first time was in September 1948 on my honeymoon with my bride Joan. We spent the first ten days of our honeymoon there and got to know the city quite well, in fact, you could say that is when I fell in love with Florence.

I have always been keenly interested in the Renaissance, and in particular the power and influence of the Medici family. Merchants, brokers, and bankers to the then known world, the Medici financed the wars of our English kings. Wherever I see the pawnbrokers sign with the three golden balls I am reminded of the Medici. The gold balls came from their coat of arms.

Arriving in Florence, it was decided that we should take a tour in an open-top bus to familiarise ourselves with the city. We then visited the various sights on foot. Heading for the Piazza della Signoria we had our first close glimpse of the church of Santa Maria dei Fiore with Brunelleschi's famous Dome. Standing alongside it is my favourite piece of Florentine architecture - Il Torre di Giotto - Giotto's wonderful campanile with its multi-coloured marbles. Next a quick visit to the Loggia dei Lanzi and the Baptistery with Ghiberti's bronze doors, Michelangelo's colossal David stands in front of the Palazzo Vecchio as if in defence of the city. We made our way past the Uffizi and PITTI palaces, the queues waiting for admittance to the art collections was horrendously long, so we made our way past the array of works by the many pavement artists along the left bank of the Arno towards the Ponte Vecchio, the only bridge over the Arno that was left undamaged during the last war. Crossing the bridge, we dragged our ladies away from the very expensive jewellery shops which line either side of the bridge! We took a short respite for a bite to eat and a glass or two of the local wine. Walking along the right bank of the Arno we noted the brown waters of the river making its way to Florence's rival city of Pisa. After a short stroll along the river bank, we climbed the tree-lined lanes to the Piazzale Michelangelo with the church of San Miniato. It is on this piazza that the young Italian brides like to pose for their photographs, with the city of Florence as a backdrop. Standing there, memories came flooding back to me when in 1948, I had stood back there with my English bride as we looked down as the setting sun caught the red roofs of the Duomo. Unfortunately, time was pressing and we had to retrace our steps for the return to San Marcello.

Brief Encounter

Our return train to San Marcello was rapidly filling up; we did manage to get seats all together in one compartment, however there was one vacant seat next to mine. After a pleasant day in Florence I relaxed looking forward to our dinner and wondered if the Zuccotto would be a success or not. The train was just drawing out of the station when she walked into our compartment. She apparently had just made it in time. She was elegant, very attractive, wearing a floral-patterned summer dress, auburn haired with lovely brown eyes. Spotting the empty seat, she gave an enquiring look in my direction as if as to say 'May I sit here?' I nodded, and helping her with her briefcase, I made room for her. She really was attractive and might as well have stepped right out the pages of Boccaccio's Decameron.

As was to have been expected, my friends immediately took the opportunity of taunting me with expressions such as, 'Look! He's at it again!' and 'Leave her alone Hector!' The lady could tell that I was slightly embarrassed and gave me a reassuring smile.

"You must excuse my friends," I said, "they always like to tease me whenever I am with an attractive lady!" I explained to her at some length that we were a group of English ramblers returning to our Hotel Giardini at San Marcello.

"I know it well," she said, "Ma come mai Lei parla italiano così bene?" she enquired. (How come you speak Italian so well?)

I explained to her that although I was born in England my parents had been Italian, having emigrated in 1919 from their home town of Bardi in the province of Parma. As children, I explained, my brothers and I grew up speaking only English, but later in life I had been determined to learn my mother's tongue and so I had enrolled in evening classes. Once I had passed my preliminary exams, my teacher had recommended I should go on for further studies. She took me to seminars and lectures at Manchester and Cardiff Universities and we would go to the opera and also watch Italian films.

"I really do admire your tenacity and determination," she said. She leant towards me conspiratorially and said "perhaps we should give your friends something to talk about! My name is Beatrice. I work in Florence as a theatrical producer." I introduced myself and so we began to make small talk. We discovered a mutual love for the arts and Florence, in particular. She confided in me her sadness that Florence was being suffocated by the hundreds of coaches disgorging hordes of tourists onto the streets of Florence:

"Like so many flocks of pigeons," she said, "they gather around their tour leader holding aloft the logo of the tour company. Follow me! Follow me! They busy themselves with their cameras. They buy their postcards, have a pizza and a cappuccino and then they're off again in their coaches only to repeat the same procedure in Lucca or Sienna!" she went on.

"Hai ragione" I conceded, but I did feel a little guilty having just done the very same thing with my friends.

"It saddens me to see Benvenuto Cellini's masterful bronze of Perseus tucked away in the Loggia dei Lanzi surrounded by lesser known works' I said. "I do feel that this masterpiece deserves a more prominent site in the city"

"You are quite right of course," she said, "but you know that we are Italians and, the Florentines in particular, have art coming out of our ears and we do take these things for granted."

"Then again," I explained, "the whole world comes to admire Michelangelo's David and very rightly so, but Donatello's David also deserves some respect!" We chatted on and on. I was enjoying this brief encounter and as she leant towards me her proximity, friendly demeanour and her perfume were beginning to cancel all my inhibitions. Gone were all my thoughts of correct grammar, I found myself talking fluently in Italian and I was really enjoying myself talking to Beatrice! The train began to slow down.

"Questa è la mia stazione", (This is my station) she said. "I have had a hard day at the studio," she continued. "All I want to do when I get home is kick off my shoes, reach for my favourite book and relax with a nice cool glass of prosecco?"

"Wish I could join you "I said.

"And why not," she replied. I could easily run you back to your hotel."

"Lei è troppo gentile", (you are too kind) I said. "But I'm afraid I must get back early to the Hotel Giardini" I explained my anxiety about the success or not of the Zuccotto I had made earlier. She rose from her seat, I handed her, her briefcase, and with the gentlest of squeezes she took my hand and said:

"Veramente è stato un vero piacere fare la Sua conoscenza!" (It has truly been a pleasure getting to know you.) As she reached the compartment door she turned and blew me a kiss, and her lips parted with a silent ciao! The seat remained empty for the remainder of the journey, but her perfume lingered on!

A brief encounter

Gala Dinner

Back at the Giardini and with our Florentine memories behind us, we took a quick shower and changed. The ladies looked their best as usual. We made for the bar, congratulating ourselves on our splendid day out in Florence. We entered the dining room, all in festive mood and looking forward to our gala dinner. There was great hilarity as the lights were dimmed and in came the two waitresses holding aloft the two Zuccotto as Pam and I bit our lower lips in apprehension. The Zuccotto was then served; however, we need not have worried. I gave it a seven out of ten, and if I had I prepared it at home, I would have given it perhaps a nine. Pam and I gave each other the thumbs up and everyone seemed pleased. The wine flowed, the talk became animated and we were all in a happy mood.

We toasted Neil and his charming wife Jill and we thanked him for his organising acumen and hoped that he would repeat another such holiday. We thanked Jock for his consummate skill and thoughtfulness in looking after us on the walks and finally we thanked Cinzia and Rudy for being such hospitable hosts. Full of good humour we retired to Rudy's disco to dance the night away.

Was it the wine I wondered? I had this wonderful dream: I was at the disco dancing with Jill and there was a tap on my shoulder, it was Cinzia,

"c' è stata una telefonata per Lei" (there was a telephone call for you) she said. "I told the caller you were at dinner. The caller said, 'do not disturb him just give him my message":

Spero che lo zuccotto è andato bene e dagli i miei più sincere auguri." (Tell him that I hope the Zuccotto was a success and give him my very best wishes.)

"She did not leave her number," Cinzia said,

"Don't worry about it, Cinzia" I replied. "This happens to me all the time!"

Departure

All too soon it was time for our departure. Our luggage was stowed away on the coach which was to take us to Bologna airport, and having said our farewells to Cinzia and Rudy we set off, taking with us happy memories and fond recollections of the fun and happy times spent at the Hotel Giardini.

Entering the town of Marzobotto en route for Bologna, we were guided through the town by the police. The whole town was bedecked with Italian flags and there were coaches bringing people into town, who seemed to be in a festive mood. This was not so, however. The crowds were in fact making for the church. I realised as we drove through that this was the annual commemoration of the day in 1944, when hundreds of men, women and children had been massacred by the SS, in reprisal for the acts of resistance carried out by the Partisans in the Tuscan hills. It was a sobering thought as we continued our journey to the airport. But we had enjoyed a very happy holiday and looked forward to our flight home; we were content as we took the flight back to Biddulph, Newcastle and Stoke-on-Trent.

Information on the massacre in Marzabotto Italy

Former SS officers sentenced for massacre in Marzabotto, Italy

More than 60 years ago, German SS units carried out a brutal massacre in the northern Italian town of Marzabotto, in which hundreds were killed. An Italian military court in La Spezia has only now sentenced, in absentia, the ten SS officers involved to life imprisonment and ordered to pay compensation of 100 million Euros to the survivors and relatives of the victims. A further seven are accused.

The massacre of the civilian population of Marzabotto, carried out between September 29 and October 1, 1944, by units of the 16th SS Armoured Infantry Division under the leadership of the notorious SS Sturmbannfuhrer Walter Reder, was the worst and most brutal Nazi crimes of the Second World War.

Some 800 people, mainly women, children and older men, were mown down and murdered in Marzabotto alone, with a further 1,000 killed in surrounding villages. The victims included some 200 children, some only a few days old.

The SS soldiers broke into houses, schools and churches, shooting their victims with machine guns, throwing hand grenades into houses and setting fire to buildings and churches. They even continued to shoot into the growing mountain of corpses. The few who survived only escaped death because they were covered by the corpses of their relatives and neighbours, or were able to hide.

A few weeks earlier, on August 12, 1944, the same SS unit, as well as Wehrmact (regular army) soldiers had just taken part in the massacre of Sant' Anna di Stazzema, which claimed 560 victims within just a few hours.

Commenting on the verdict, a member of the Association of the Relatives of the Marzabotto Victims said, "Justice has prevailed at last. We waited decades for this verdict."

Cinque Terre; seniors take steps in Italy by Liz Tomlinson

Twenty ramblers from the Stoke and Newcastle Group enjoyed an exhilarating Ramblers Holiday in the Cinque Terre and Ligurian Alps in Italy in September 2007. The holiday was efficiently organised by Mavis Heath, and expertly led by Rambler's Holidays leader Mike Harding and his wife Pat. 'Super Steve' Heath provided practical help and support throughout the holiday.

The gregarious group, ranging in age from a mere 58 years to a fit and famous Hector Emannuellie at 87 years, flew to Pisa and continued by coach to Sestri Levante, their first base. This small seaside resort lies north of the five fishing villages that make up the unique area known as the Cinque Terre, a national park of stunning beauty and amazing villages clinging to cliffs that rise vertically from the sea. Here a network or paths crisscross the ancient terraces and drop and climb in and out of the five villages.

A railway line services the precipitous area and the group used this convenient transport daily to make one or another of the picturesque villages their starting point. Preparing for fabulous costal views, the group were surprised to find that most of the journey was through long, rock-hewn tunnels with only the occasional flash of Mediterranean and blue sky. Most days the group would set out together and then split into two or three groups to vary the demands of the day. Vernazza was the bustling beginning, to the walk south to Corniglia and Manarola along the Sentiero Azzurro, the Blue path. Riomaggiore, the furthest village, was the springboard for a strenuous walk south of the Cinque Terre to Porto venere. Both these walks began with record-breaking step climbing that tested knees and endurance, and only the thought of an Italian Ice cream carried some to the end! The climb out of Riomaggiore was approximately 1,300 steps - quite a springboard that took the walkers high above the Mediterranean and the cliff-clinging villages, with views to die for [and they nearly did!] A walk from Monterosso, the most northerly village, began with a corkscrew taxi ride that Alton Towers would envy! Up and up, out of the village to begin a fabulous walk slowly descending to Vernazza, spotting numerous wild flowers on the way and always stunned by the views. The anticipated drop into the village was steep and lengthy along cobbled tracks and the tops of terrace walls, and then a picnic on the harbour wall while Super Steve had a swim with the bikini-clad Italian mermaids! Worth carrying a cozzie Steve!

Each walk was an aerobic workout in glorious sunshine. The paths up and down between villages and terraces are carved out of steep hillsides, many are vertical flights of steps of varying width, height and condition....and endless. The paths along the terrace walks are often vertiginous, the descents frequently precarious, but this group are not wimps! Sun hats, knee supports and alpine poles protected and supported them; and the magnificent views of sweeping sea and coloured clustered houses were just reward and much photographed. The homeward trains were packed with holidaymakers, many

walkers with rucksacks and boots because this area is popular with Americans and other Europeans.

Outside the Hotel at Santo Stefano

The non-walking day at Sestri happened to be Hector's 87th birthday, and the group celebrated with a train ride north to Santa Margherita and a picturesque sail into Portofino, the famous celebrity hang-out. Portofino is small, pretty and very, very expensive. Dinner that evening included birthday-cake and

Prosecco. Hector even sat in a balloon-bedecked chair and looked very proud. And so he should!

On the eighth day, the group left the busy coastal region and headed for the Ligurian hills and the ancient town of Varese Ligure, interestingly built to the circular design in the 12th century. The borgo Rotondo was a means of defence and the sweeping curve of the old houses is still clearly evident. The group spent two nights here allowing them to take walks on high pastures with more wonderful views. On leaving Varese, one group went ahead to walk a ridge - more fabulous views, while a second group strolled and took coffee and pizza before joining the walkers to drive to the Apennine Mountains for their first base.

Santo Stefano D'Aveto is a ski resort and a peaceful and pleasant walking base with many way-marked paths. There is an impressive castle ruin at the centre of this modern resort and the alpine feel to the geranium clad houses and shops. The air is clean and fresh and the sun less harsh, and so the group enjoyed an ideal walking climate. Public transport and a local mini coach were used and many walks were possible from the hotel. Again, the group reformed into two smaller groups to give choice of pace and destination. The walking was either up or down! Not a lot of 'along', and so again there were breathtaking views. Wild flowers and bell-ringing cows were in abundance.

Hector organised a treat for the non-walking day - an amazing coach ride through the mountains to Bardi, the hometown of his parents and grandparents. The entire group participated in this nostalgic day as Hector took his friends to see a roadside cappella of family significance, and to a tiny village where the New York Sidoli family are responsible for the shining marble floor. Treated like royalty, the group were met in Bardi and escorted to the Council Chambers for an official greeting from the Mayor. After wining and dining at the local hostelry, a tour of the medieval castle was awe-inspiring; it is so huge and so well maintained. An impressive display in English as well as in Italian explained the migration of the people from the area in the 20th century, of which Hector's parents

With Mavis (The Baptistery at Ceresto)

were but two. Everyone had a wonderful day, not least of all an emotional Hector.

Thanks to Mavis and Steve, Mike and Pat and Hector, the group returned with rucksacks bursting with digital photos and happy memories. There's nothing quite like sharing an amazing holiday with friends!

Liz Tomlinson

www.ramblersholidays.co.uk

September 13 Portugal 2008

It is now the first few days of January 2012. It was a cold and frosty morning and a group of us, all members of the Stoke and Newcastle Ramblers' Association were having a welcome coffee break during the course of one of our walks. The hiatus of the Christmas and New Year celebrations had come and gone and the subject of the summer holidays came up: during past years, we usually took a week's walking holiday, often during September or early October. We had in the past walked in Scotland, Wales, the Lake District, the Yorkshire Dales, the Isle of Man, the Isle of Wight, and the Austria and Italian Dolomites. During the discussion my mind went back to the same time of the year, four years earlier. It was 2008 when Mavis Heath, a member of our group, announced that we were to travel to Portugal for a two-week holiday exploring and walking the Douro Valley. This delighted me immensely as in October 1955 I had attended an exhibition of Portuguese Art at the Royal

Academy in London. I had taken two days off from the family business. The exhibition was promoted by the Portuguese Government and covered all aspects of Portuguese art ranging from paintings, statuary and furniture to ceramics and silverware. It was very well attended, but at the time I never thought that I would someday visit Portugal.

On September 13, 2008 thirteen of us, all members of the Stoke and Newcastle Ramblers' Association, set off from Manchester airport bound for Portugal and the Douro Valley. Mavis had organised our transfer to the airport by mini bus, however, despite many phone calls and correspondence with Ramblers Holidays, our flight, which should have taken us to Oporto, was redirected to Frankfurt, where we had to transfer to a flight to Lisbon. This delay was of course very exasperating and we were all very tired and not looking forward to the long coach ride along the country roads to our hotel at Oporto.

Arriving at Lisbon airport - not I must admit in the best of moods - our spirits were immediately lifted when we met the guide who was to escort us for the next two weeks walking and sightseeing along the Douro Valley. Her name was Tina; red-haired, ebullient and suntanned Tina kept us entertained and lifted our spirits along the long ride back to Oporto. Fluent in the Portuguese language and customs of the Portuguese people, she established an immediate rapport with us and it was evident that this was indeed going to be a memorable holiday. It was dark when we eventually arrived at our destination. As we crossed the overhead road we looked down to the river Douro below, the banks of the river on both sides brilliantly lit, the lights of the many restaurants and cafe bars reflected in the water of the Douro. Our coach carefully wound its way through the many squares and narrow streets of the city until we reached our hotel. We were, of course, too late for dinner but the ever-resourceful Tina soon got us organised and walked us to a well-lit piazza in the city where we were soon accommodated at the local restaurant. We sat under a full harvest moon in the balmy evening air and enjoyed our first Portuguese hospitality, chatting with the locals and being entertained by an unexpected group of young university students, immaculate in their black gowns. They were celebrating their start of term as they played their guitars and sang to us their folk songs. It was indeed a very auspicious start to our holiday. It was very late when we got to bed that first evening and were all very tired, but well content. We were staying at the Great Western INCA hotel and were to spend the first three days of our holiday here. The hotel was very comfortable and welcoming. After breakfast Tina informed us that we would spend these few days exploring and familiarising ourselves with the city. It was a glorious Sunday morning when - dutifully following Tina's footsteps - we made our way along the cobbled streets to what Tina describes as Oporto's Sunday market. Situated in one of the main City squares, it was not at all what I had envisaged. The whole market was devoted to the sale of caged birds of every description, song birds, hunting birds, exotic pets and all kinds of ancillary equipment was on display. There was a great sense of activity as buyers took home purchases in shoe boxes and tiny cages. It seems that this went on every Sunday morning.

Now I must ask my readers to excuse me. I have never kept a daily diary and the events I am about to describe may well be out of sequence. I do recall that Tina issued us with a street map with the instructions

"Now go out and have fun!"

A group of us decided to take the tram to the port of Gaia, at the mouth of the Douro where it meets the Atlantic. The tram, as I recall, was very ancient and the tram driver was even more ancient. We travelled along at speed whilst the carriage swayed from side to side until, thankfully, we arrived at our destination. After a quick coffee and ice cream to recover, we made our way to the shoreline and so decided that we would walk back along the shores of the river until we reached Oporto. It was a gloriously sunny afternoon as we made our way, passing many anglers as they waited patiently for their catches. On our right, we passed now abandoned warehouses bearing the names of famous Port wine labels; on the opposite bank of the river there were fishermen's cottages, the roofs hosting flocks of herons, evidence that the river waters were well stocked with fish.

We reached Oporto in good time having spent a very rewarding day. We then had a leisurely bite to eat before making our way back to our hotel. Thank you, Tina, for the map provided! We dined well that evening and the wine kept flowing, no sooner were the bottles emptied, they were immediately replaced without request or charge whilst Tina brought me a glass of port wine, as distinct from the dinner wine which we had been drinking.

"Try this," she said. It was of course very special. As we know port wine - like sherry or the Sicilian marsala - has a higher alcohol content than the usual dinner wine. I thanked her at the same time, remonstrating that I would like to return the compliment and buy her a drink in return. But she would have none of it as she explained. "No this is your holiday and I want you to enjoy it." By the end of the holiday I had become quite addicted. The next morning Tina explained we were to do some sightseeing in the morning and in the afternoon - by special arrangement - pay a visit to Sandemans's Porto Cellars in Oporto.

Região Demarcada do Douro

We visited several fine churches, fine town squares with their statues and medieval buildings, in particular the famous Stock Exchange, now no longer used as a Stock Exchange but used for city functions, weddings etc. It is lavishly decorated with paintings, gilt framed mirrors and chandeliers.

"You must come back next year." Tina said to me "We shall hold your birthday party here." An appointment however, that I was unable to keep. Portugal of course is a Roman Catholic country, but as Tina explained there is still an element of paganism practiced by some adherents. This was evidenced by the contents of the shop window which displayed reproductions of human organs such as hearts, livers, lungs, arms, legs and feet. They were used in certain rites together with prayers to the Virgin Mary requesting cures, so keeping their faith in both camps. There were other specialist shops that dealt only in particular trades; one such shop only sold zip-fasteners, but of every description, another traded in locks and keys, another in buttons, another in ribbons. This, it seems was not a throwaway society and whatever one needs, it could be found here.

At the appointed hour we all assembled at the entrance to Sandemans Porto Cellars on the banks of the Douro. Sandemans is, of course, only one of many famous port-wine names. It is the most well-known although many claim that some of the much less-known brands are superior. Oporto and the port of Gaia is the commercial centre of the port-wine industry and it is in the cellars of Oporto and Gaia that the wine is aged and stored before being exported worldwide to an ever more discriminating consumer. Since Roman times, man has cultivated and nurtured the upper reaches of the Douro Valley, planting vineyards on the hillsides of both banks of the Douro. The famous *vinho verde* and other well-known Portuguese wines are also produced here.

As we entered the cellars we were greeted by a very charming English speaking guide who gave us a brief history of the Sandeman Company and many facts and figures regarding the volume of production, vintages, sizes of the vats and so on, which I must confess are now all a blur to me. I was, however, very impressed by the size and spaciousness of the cathedral like rooms that led on into the hillside. Huge vats the size of double-decker buses. Who - I wondered - would drink all this port wine? Our little group had halted for a moment while we examined a particular vat.

Our Sandeman guide meanwhile walked off slowly with measured step into the gloomy interior of the vast cathedral-like interior, her black, ankle length gown swaying side to side, on her head the little coquettish Spanish hat, the perfect feminine reproduction of the famous Sandemans logo which is printed on each bottle of their port: I was impressed and I thought to myself, one day I will paint that image. Hurrying forward we soon caught up with our guide and very soon we entered the brightly lit reception area, where tables were laid out with glass after glass of every type and vintage of port wine. This time it was not Tina who encouraged me to sample each vintage, but our charming Sandeman guide. I tasted - or should I say - I drank my fill and came to the conclusion that perhaps after all, those that criticised Sandemans port were unfair. Yes, I thought to myself, when I get back to the UK I shall certainly try to capture and paint that image of the retreating figure as she vanished into the dimness of the vat-lined cellars carved into the Douro hillside. We emerged into the bright sunshine and walked along the promenade admiring the restored ancient barques which in olden times would bring down from the upper reaches of the Douro casks of wine from the numerous vineyards to be stored in the many cellars in which the wine was aged for export all over the world.

Our three-day visit to Porto had taught us a lot about Portuguese life and customs and although we had not done any serious walking we agreed that we had a wonderful time. At the end of each day's excursion we would wander down to the shore line and walk along the riverside in the warm balmy atmosphere, mixing with the locals and admiring the cruise ships which were well lit up and anchored along the shore.

We made our way slowly up the hill through now familiar squares and cobbled streets to the hotel. We were looking forward to a well-earned dinner. Tina informed us that tomorrow we should be leaving Oporto for Miranda de Douro, the next stage of our holiday, where we would do some serious walking. I was not surprised when Tina brought me a night cap - a glass of port of course!

Miranda Do Douro

Our itinerary decreed that we were to spend the next five days at Miranda do Douro, a small medieval town and the source of the river Douro. We made an early departure from the hotel and arrived at the main station where we were to take the train to Pinocchio. Steve, Mavis's husband, helped us older members with handling and heaving our luggage aboard the train. We were fascinated and left lost in admiration by the vast entrance hall, the wall of which was completely covered in titles depicting scenes of biblical and historical events, partly obscured by scaffolding, the titles or *azulejos* were in the course of being cleaned, but the impression was indeed memorable. Everywhere we went we were to see examples of the Portuguese love of tiling.

The rail journey - as on most Portuguese railways - was slow, but this gave us ample opportunity to admire the wonderful views of the vineyards that covered the hillside; and to admire the sleepy little villages we passed with their miniature railway stations and once again a host of building with tiled walls. We arrived in good time and were welcomed at the Hotel Residencial Planalto.

Here Steve repeated his good deed with the luggage. After we had settled in there was an hour or two to spare, so I ventured into the historical centre of the town and paid a visit to the Museu da Terra de Miranda. This small museum was opened in 1982 by Father Antonio Mountinho, an enthusiast and lover of local society and culture. Father Mountinho promoted Miranda de Douro with his knowledge of historic, archaeological, linguistic and ethnological undertakings. These facts were given to me by an enthusiastic young curator who insisted in taking me around the museum room by room. She was eager, she said, to improve her understanding and practice of the English language. Each room in succession was rich in artefacts relating to the daily life and rituals of the past. Ancient farming and agricultural implement, kitchen and domestic utensils, basketry and field traps denoting the need to protect the crops from pests and predators with ancient handlooms for the production of linen and woollen garments. Of particular interest was the Capa de Honras Mirandesa, (Cape of Honour) used in certain ceremonies in Miranda. There were masks of leather and wood favoured by the young men of the district during Christmas and other festivities. This was a very interesting collection for this small historical museum. As I left, the young curator thanked me for helping her with her English.

"Come again," she said and "Bring your friends." Then she explained to me that the local people spoke a local dialect called Mirandese.

"Perhaps," I said, "that is why I have difficulty understanding the people here." She gave me a wry smile and then went on to explain that during the Spanish inquisition many Jews fled across the border into Miranda do Douro, settling into their new homes, they would hang imitation hams and pork sausages from their balcony windows, thus denoting that they were pork eaters and not Jews, so avoiding any possible hostile reaction. Our hotel was not as luxurious as the hotel Oporto but it was clean and the food was good. After all is said and done, we ramblers do not always want five-star luxury when on a walking holiday.

During our five days at Miranda, Tina escorted us on many fine walks, through gorges, ravines, the vineyards, and tiny villages and country lanes of the area. We grew to learn the difference between fig, almond, olive, walnut trees and the occasional cork tree which is sadly in decline as the wine bottlers begin to use plastic corks. We were welcomed wherever we went and Tina always saw to it that I had my customary glass of Port wine. I can recall one very hot, sunny morning in particular; we had stopped to allow Margaret Cox to catch us up. Margaret, a keen botanist would often stop, going down on her hands and knees to examine a particular flower or plant. It was very often that she was unable to identify it!

Continuing our walk, we came to a farm and it was evident that Tina knew the young farmer. He invited us into his barn where we were able to enjoy the shade and rest a while. He introduced us to his herd of Mirandese cows with their cute little calves. The Mirandese is a special breed and it was evident that he was very proud of them, they were well groomed with large glamorous eyes and lashes and they were indeed very fine beasts. Whilst we were there many farm cats raced around and played among the bales of hay.

Grateful for this pleasant interlude and rest we continued on our walk. It was later in the afternoon that I was to experience what seemed to me to be a vision. We came upon a clearing on the arid plateau, a small brackish-looking pool, a herd of not-too-clean looking sheep, and there on a slight rise stood this tall, majestic figure, the sun behind his back, bearded with a long ankle length robe of dun coloured material, standing there immobile with his long shepherd's crook. It was a truly biblical apparition. We continued along the path to a stone wall on one side, thorny bushes on the other. Suddenly the herd of sheep came rushing through, forcing us to shelter against the wall. It was followed by the tall figure of the shepherd; he looked straight ahead, never spoke a word and disappeared into the distance taking his flock to pastures new. I wondered, did he perhaps consider us to be part of his flock? The vision, if it was a vision, still haunts me to this day.

Continuing our walk, we came upon a tourist sign to "A shrine to Our Lady." Tina explained that it was only a short detour from our committed path and so we dutifully followed her. Apparently, this shrine was not very often visited these days, she said, as pilgrims favour the shrine at Fatima. This is evidently so because as we approached we saw that the once well-paved pathways are now covered with weeds and there is an apparent sense of neglect. The once splendid rows of rose bushes were in poor condition. The one redeeming feature however is the Holy well, which was still in a good state, and there we were able to refill our water bottles and drink the cool refreshing water. Tina took me to one side and insisted in helping me to bathe my maculate diseased eyes with the holy water. A silent prayer to our Lady, but there was no miraculous cure! We re-joined the original path and within a short walk we reached our village rendezvous where we enjoyed our coffee, cake and a glass of Port wine.

On yet another occasion, Tina promised us that for our lunch-time stop we were to enjoy a barbeque lunch. After a rather gruelling morning walk and feeling tired, we came across what for the world looked very much like a western cowboy type of establishment. There in the hot sun were wooden tables all laid out for us with the barbeque blazing and in no time at all we were all tucking into roast sausages, chops and home-baked bread with ample draughts of red wine. The atmosphere was very jolly and we had a splendid time. The feasting over, it was time to dance. It seemed, however, that our hosts were only familiar with the flute and pipes and so I am afraid that we were not very good at the dancing, we left the 'ranch' however in good spirits.

Tina explained that there was a retired farmer in the village who had converted his house and farm into a living museum and that she thought it would be a good idea to pay him a visit. This we did, and for me especially, it was a real eye opener. The ancient artefacts and farm implements reminded me of the time that I spent at the tender age of seven when I visited my grandfather's farm in the Apennines of Northern Italy. My mother had taken me there in 1927 and this visit brought it all back to me. I explained this to the gentleman, with the aid of Tina's translation and I told him that he reminded me of my grandfather, he was delighted, and this of course resulted in toasting 'old timers' with several glasses of wine.

I had drunk quite a lot at the barbeque and when the old gentleman gave me a final glass of grappa I was not at all steady on my feet. Grappa is a forty percent liqueur which is distilled from the skins and residue, after the grapes have been trod.

We left the farm and continued on our way; the sun was very hot. I had had too much to drink, and I realised that I was not waking in a straight line. I was wandering and not keeping up with the others. I just had to sit down for a while. I think it was Joan and Mavis who came to my side and asked if I was alright, they gave me lots of water to drink and after a while I felt well enough to continue the rest of the walk. Tina admonished me and saw to it that I took frequent drinks of water and I resolved to be more temperate in the future. That evening before dinner Tina reminded us that on the morrow we would be leaving Miranda for the next stage of our holiday, we would be leaving for Régua.

Régua

We left Miranda travelling by rail and road and Steve once again helped the older members of the group with their luggage. We would spend five nights at Régua, where we stayed at the Imperio Hotel. Régua is the capital of the Upper Douro Valley and the commercial centre of the port wine industry. Here we would be able to visit the vineyards and experience first-hand, man's impact on the landscape, his expertise in viniculture aided by the combination of the soil, the choice of grape varieties, and the glorious sunshine that culminates in the production of port and table wines of world-class quality.

It was in this area that we did some serious walking. We had left the somewhat arid area of the Mirandese plateau and now walked through the villages and vineyards, always in bright sunshine. Does it ever rain,

I thought, in Portugal? Wherever we went we always met with the most generous hospitality and each time we stopped at a cafe bar, Tina would disappear behind the counter and emerge with my customary glass of port. It was apparent that she was spoiling me, this was becoming increasingly embarrassing, but I must admit that I enjoyed it.

Several of the walks that we took in this area still stand out in my memory and I shall try to recollect them for you. You will excuse me if they are not in chronological order, but after four years and a diminishing memory I shall do my best.

One particular morning with the help of two taxis Tina took us to the summit of a local mountain, the name of which now escapes me. This, in splendid isolation, was what appeared to be a deserted chapel adjacent to a large rock. Tina explained that it was the custom with the local mothers-to-be or young brides to gather here in expectation of favours. It was claimed that the rock has some mystical or religious powers however Tina explained to take it with a pinch of salt. She went on to tell us that from this spot we would take a ten-mile walk, but - smiling - she added that it was all downhill. But as we walkers realised, downhill walking is not always the easiest. We descended gradually, passing through delightful hillside villages, past barking dogs, geranium-clad balconies and endless hillside villages. One such vineyard with a perilous downward slope which required extra care; we needed to walk in single file as the soil was falling away from our feet down the steep slope whilst we held on the crumbling stone wall on our left. We all made it safely however, as we emerged eventually on to a firmer path before entering the village.

Unfortunately, once again the name of this remote village escapes me. We entered the village through a passage, with a wall clad with a climbing rose on our right. It was like we were leaving the wings of a theatre stage right into what was the perfect stage setting of an operatic village. In bright sunlight, centre stage was a group of housewives doing their washing in the large water trough, groups of ladies were chatting, and children were playing whilst some of the men of the village offered us fresh figs and other delicacies. It was as if we had wandered into the production of a Puccini opera, all that was missing was the music. We tarried here a while and even helped some of the ladies with their washing. It brought to my mind an Old Italian folk song where the lover sings to his lady: I'll give you a rough translation of the ditty.

"I have washed your 'kerchief in the fountain

I have washed it with soap and water,

In the bright sunshine I have laid it out to dry

On the rose bush standing by,

I have pressed it with loving care,

Each fold I press with love in my heart

I return it to you unseen by your mother and father."

We said farewell to our friendly villagers and made our way downhill. I pictured in my mind the theatre curtain coming down and closing the act. Tina later confided in me that most of the villagers had their own washing machine but preferred to do their washing in public where they could exchange gossip and so on. I did wonder at the time whether Tina had prearranged or advised the villagers of our impending arrival as it seemed that she was known to several of the ladies. Tina, I am sure, would make a superb theatrical producer!

Continuing our downhill walk, we eventually arrived at an establishment which was run by three sisters. They were preparing for the grape harvest, which would be carried out the following week. The vineyard had its own church, which was a fine baroque building which one of the sisters took great pleasure in showing us around. Another of the sisters talked to us about the family history of the establishment and the production of port wine. The third sister was busily engaged in carryout repairs to their bottling plant; they bottled their own wine here, however she explained that unfortunately, they did not export to

England. We spent some time tasting their dinner and port wines. In this instance, I can remember the name of the village institution because one of the sisters gave me their visiting card. It was called Quinta Santa du Euphemia. Within a short while we had reached the foot of the mountain and after a most memorable day we made our way to our hotel.

It is true that while we were staying at Miranda do Douro and also Régua we had enjoyed many exhilarating and sometimes even arduous walks, but it was not all walking and no play. We made several excursions and sightseeing trips into the surrounding countryside. One such trip was to the casa de Mateus, a historic mansion close to the town of Vila Real. The Casa de Mateus was built in the first half of the 18th century by António José Botelho Marão (1688-1746,) the third Morgado de Mateus. The chapel was finished by his son Luís António. The architecture of the house, Portuguese baroque, is attributed to the famous Italian designer Nicolai Masoni. It reconciles the dimensions of the Portuguese noble house with the baroque exuberance displayed in the main facade whilst the decorative motifs of the roofs and the chapel were designed by Master Jose Alvarez Rego. The entrance hall and six rooms of the south wing together with four rooms of the north wing are open to the public. Two of the four rooms in the south wing were converted into a museum and contain nearly two thousand parchments and royal charters, the oldest dating from the 15th century. In the second room were the liturgical vestments with which the chapel was opened in 1759. There is a collection of silver reliquaries, a 17th wood cut altar and ivory images of Our Lady, together with other images and curiosities of a religious nature whilst the other rooms contain examples of French, Portuguese and English furniture. Also on exhibition were family portraits, silver and chinaware from the East India Company. Worthy of note were the ceilings chestnut carvings. In the chapel you can admire sculptures in wood and stone from the 16th to 18th centuries. The ceiling of the sacristy is covered with 17th century paintings representing religious figures. Amongst the silverware that was on exhibition, I thought that I recognised examples that I saw when I visited the exhibition of Portuguese Art at the Royal Academy in London way back in 1955. But in all probability I COULD BE MISTAKEN.

Unlike England, Portugal has no equivalent National Trust, as is the case in most European countries. Casa de Mateus rests in the hands of the Fundación Casa de Mateus, which is one of the most active cultural organisations in the country acting at the national and international levels. The foundation hosts concerts, training facilities, seminars and similar events. The foundation was created in 1970 by Don Francisco de Sousa Botelho de Albuquerque, conde de Mangualde, Vila Real y Melo and it is responsible for the preservation and study of the house, its activities and the promotion of cultural, scientific, and educational activities. Important effects have been made towards the restoration of the house while adapting it for present day's functions. The old barn has been converted into a concert hall with rooms for the artists; the old wood house and the old kitchen and in the upper floors of the cellars, where wine is produced are installed rooms and facilities for guests. The old olive presses and distillery have been preserved and converted into artists' residences.

Sonia, our English-speaking guide who escorted us through the various rooms of the house, was very friendly and informative. She had a wonderful sense of humour, especially when she described to us the religious relics with her tongue-in-cheek remarks. I thought she was the combination of Victoria Wood and Dawn French.

Having concluded the tour of the house, Sonia directed us to the gardens, which are considered to be among the finest in all of Portugal. Very well preserved and improved during the course of generations, they were fabulous addition to the Casa de Mateus. The granite water mirror in front of the house, the three-tiered pools fed by spring water, the tunnel of cedars in the garden designed in topiaries of different sizes were added in the middle of the 20th century to the secular camellia gardens, the monumental cedars and the magnificent threshing floor with a view of the Serra do Marão. Of particular interest was the magnificent knot garden; a very pleasant way to end our visit to the noble Casa de Mateus.

We finished our day trip by visiting the nearby town of Vila Real. Having spent longer than anticipated at the Casa de Mateus we did not have a lot of time at Vila Real. In any case it was siesta time, and most of the shops were closed. We would have liked to have been able to spend more time there, but we made use of what time there was. Vila Real is a very attractive town and would warrant much closer inspection. Time was pressing however, and it was soon time to retrace our steps back to the hotel.

Vila Real - Portugal

Lamego

On another of our walking free days we visited the town of Lamego. A charming, red-roofed town full of historic and cultural interest. As usual, our first port of call was the tourist information office, where Tina furnished us with street maps and her usual instruction:

"Now go and have fun," this of course after having highlighted the street plan with the designated place and time for regrouping and return to Regúa. Lamego is famous for one of the finest sanctuaries in all of Europe, the Santuário de Nossa Senhora do Remédios. It lies at the top of a very steep rise at the far end of the town and several of us made our way there, walking the length of the town along the tree lined boulevard with its many attractive bars and shops. Others decided to visit the craft shops and museums. It was a very steep climb to the entrance of the Sanctuary which was approached by a series of granite balustrade steps, flanking on each side, blue and white titles as we reached each stage of the climb. The wall tiles depicted biblical scenes each one different from the others. There must have been eight or nine of these stages until we finally reached the piazza in front of the basilica. We were out of breath as we enjoyed the panorama of the red roofs of the town below and the surrounding countryside. We were amazed to see Margaret Cox waiting there! She had beaten us to it; nothing could stop this 88 year old veteran! As we entered the church a kindly gentleman approached us, he appeared to be the custodian and with his broken English he offered to conduct us around the Sanctuary.

Lamego - Portugal

With his broken English, some French and a little Italian he explained to us the history, the many works of art and artefacts of the fine baroque building.

Unfortunately, time was pressing and we had to make our way back down the many flights of steps to the town below. We made our way back along the boulevard to where we were to meet up with Tina. We were in good time however, and as we approached the meeting point I noticed Tina just around a corner, sitting at a bar reading and enjoying her customary cigarette. I joined her, a quick drink, and a chat and then we joined the waiting group. It had been yet another enjoyable and happy day! But there was more to come!

Riva Lungo

Before dinner that evening Tina announced that the following day would be our last walking day of the holiday, but, she resumed, it will be a day that you remember.

"We are going to climb to the remote mountain-top of Riva Lungo." This she explained would involve a train journey on the famous narrow gauge railway, which Michael Palin describes as one of his favourite train rides. After breakfast, we made our way down to the railway station where we crossed the tracks into the narrow gauge line. Two ancient carriages were there ready for us. We filled one carriage together with some locals. The carriage had plain wooden seats, but large windows which allowed us ample opportunity to view the magnificent scenery as we climbed the ever-ascending serpentine bends. There were hills completely covered in vineyards, the rows of vines alternating into a pattern of horizontal, vertical, and diagonal strips. The scene changed constantly as we rounded each bend. There were occasional glimpses of movement among the vines as peasants were busily engaged in the picking and harvesting of the grapes.

Eventually, we reached the end of the line. We had arrived at the village strangely named 'short trousers.'

You might think this is a strange name for a hamlet remotely situated in the hills of Regúa. The explanation is quite simple: the landlord of the local inn is a man of very short temper and very argumentative; whenever he finds himself at the point when he is losing the argument he loses his temper, he bangs his fist on the table or slams down the phone and he explodes with the declamation. "Do you think I am still in short trousers?" And so, the village is always referred to as Short Trousers!

We left the train and made our way to the inn eager to refresh ourselves with perhaps cold drinks, coffee etc. At the same time, we were joined by a group of mountain bikers helmeted and nylon clad. The sudden surge of custom confirmed to us that the landlord was indeed not very hospitable as most of the Portuguese that we met were. He was indeed very grumpy as he was behest with demands for our various needs. Coffee with hot milk please, cafe latte please, black coffee no sugar, diet coke please. He was completely flustered, and I was expecting him at any moment to lose his temper and exclaim "So you think I am still in short trousers?"

The situation was saved however. Tina soon found herself behind the bar and all were eventually served. I saw her catch the landlord's ear, he bent down and from under the bar he produced a bottle. Then Tina joined me with two glasses of Port wine - on the house of course! And so suitably refreshed we set off on what was to be the long and arduous climb to the village of Riva Lungo. The afternoon was swelteringly hot and the going was tough. Along stony and dusty paths we passed through several vineyards where Steve took several bunches of grapes, which we all shared. The farmer, I'm sure would not have objected. Steadily climbing we took advantage of what little shade came our way. I found myself alone with Tina. She made me take a long drink of water; we talked in the shadows, we talked of this and that, of things in our past. Still climbing, we reached the outskirts of the village. We rested on the doorsteps of the village houses and then after a long and tiring climb we were in the village centre. We had made it! Hot, tired and thirsty we all gathered there, thankful that we had reached the end of our walk. Tina ushered us into the front room of the nearby house; it was a very small room and all thirteen of us soon filled it.

The well-scrubbed wooden farm house tables were all laid out with fresh green salads, fruit, and home-baked bread and on each table were several two litre bottles of Coca Cola. At least we thought it was Coca Cola until Mavis who was very thirsty took a draught only to find that they contained red wine! We ate off of paper plates and cups, but this true Portuguese hospitality did not surprise us. Tina introduced me to the host and hostess who were it seems the proprietors of the local farm and vineyard. We all had a most enjoyable time and then we were invited to visit their village church, which was being redecorated. Several of the village ladies accompanied us and then we were invited to help them tread the grapes, which had only recently been harvested. With only a few exceptions, we readily agreed. There were three huge vats; the one on the left was already occupied by two burly young farmers busily treading; they trod, their arms crossed, in rhythmic unison, each one doing a figure of eight. With measured steps, they never spoke but continued as if every step was choreographed. True professionalism! We discarded our boots and socks, tucked our outer wear into our knickers, in case of the ladies, and were helped into the middle of the three vats. There was great merriment and laughter as we trod the grapes without any sort of rhythm, while the two young men on our right looked on us with amusement, as we amateurs kept bumping into each other. Even our 88 year old Margaret Cox took part, and it brought to my mind the stories that my mother told me of the days when as a young girl on her father's farm in Italy she took part in treading the grapes and of the fun they had at what was called the "vendemmia," the time of the grape harvest. The grapes that we had trod I was told were destined to be bottled under the Taylor's label. It was an honour to have been asked to tread those grapes and a wonderful experience to boot, an experience I for one would not have missed for the world. With some assistance we got out of the vat and with well-stained legs we emerged into the farm yard where the ladies washed us down with hose pipes and towelled us dry. This caused much laughter and ribaldry.

Tina had told us that this was going to be a day that we would remember and she had certainly kept her word. But it was not over yet, as we were to find out, there was more to come. Reluctantly leaving this charming village we made our way to the roadside where we were to await our transport to take us down from the mountain, back to our hotel in Regúa. We waited for a while, but no coach it seemed, was forthcoming. Then a motorised, flat bedded farm truck arrived.

"Right," said Tina "all aboard!" We were made to lie on our backs facing each other across the bare boards of the truck, like many tinned sardines. Tina sat above us, her back against the cab. She sat there like Queen Boudicca, her Kaftan blouse catching the breeze as we swept down the mountain side at ever-increasing speed as we rounded each sharp bend of the road. There were screams and there were silent prayers that the brakes would hold. Alton Towers could not have given us a more thrilling, and even frightening experience. Tina had certainly kept her promise and this was indeed a day that we would never forget. We arrived at Regúa with shaking legs and made our way with rather ungainly steps to our hotel.

Showered and refreshed we went down to dinner that evening in the full knowledge that once again Tina had given us a day to remember. The exhilarating ride down the mountain side was without doubt the perfect climax to a wonderful holiday. It was agreed that Tina had without doubt managed the day's activities with true professional expertise. We had much to talk about that evening at dinner, however it was to be our last evening at the Hotel Imperio. Tomorrow morning, we were to leave for Oporto where we were to spend one last night at the Great Western Hotel before catching our plane back to England in the afternoon. The dinner as usual went well, we had reached the coffee stage when Tina took me aside and explained that she had bought a bouquet of flowers which she intended to present to the chef in recognition of the fine meals we had enjoyed during our stay.

"I would like you to do the presentation," she said. I demurred.

"I do not know the language," I explained

"That is no problem," she insisted. "I shall translate for you." Reluctantly I agreed, and the chef was called for. The chef turned out to be a rather buxom and jolly lady; handing her the bouquet I thanked her on behalf of the group for the excellent meals which we had enjoyed whilst Tina translated. She thanked me and said that it had been a pleasure catering for such happy guests, Tina again translated and then there were hugs and kisses and it was all over. However, I need not have worried, as before retiring I lingered for a while with Tina at the bar where we sat and talked over a glass or two of port wine. On the following day we were to leave early, with our bags packed for our last night at the great Western Hotel in Oporto.

We checked in at the hotel after breakfast, and spent most of the day visiting old haunts, and the places that had caught our attention during the first three days of our holiday. The weather was still very hot and sunny, and we wondered what the weather would be like back home. We strolled along the river side with some doing a little shopping for presents and postcards. We stopped for coffees at our favourite bars, but I supposed we were all rather thoughtful, realising that our holiday was at its end. We made our way, loitering, up the hill through familiar narrow streets to our hotel where we made an early start packing our things before going down to dinner. This was to be our last evening dinner in Portugal. At dinner that evening we talked about the many happy days we had spent, the wonderful walks, our visit to the Casa de Mateus, the Sanctuary at Lamego, the visit to Sandeman's port Cellars and many other wine tastings, the grape treading at Riva Lungo, Short trousers and the mountain railway journey and - as the climax - the ride down the mountain side. All experiences that we would never forget. At dinner that evening Tina and I sat opposite each other. Was that sadness I saw in her eyes? Her hand reached out and finding mine we toasted each other. The dinner was over, I rose and gave thanks to Mavis for organising this holiday in the first instance; I thanked Steve, her husband for willingly helping with the handling of our luggage. Finally, I thanked Tina for so wonderfully giving us a holiday that we would never forget. I handed her a single red rose which I think meant more to her than a bouquet of flowers. She was visibly moved. Now back at home in Stoke-on-Trent, four years have gone by. I can still recall those happy days spent in the Valley of the Douro. Tina and I are still in touch. Birthday and Christmas cards. I still drink a glass of port wine now and then. It helps to raise one's spirits! Many happy thoughts come flooding back of the days spent in the Valley of the Douro. And so, dear reader, you might come across me one of these days, at Sainsbury's supermarket, most likely in the wines and spirits department. I will be scanning the port wine section, all the well-known brands will be there, Sandeman, Offley, the Rozi, the Cruz, but I shall be looking particular for Taylor's, and in particular for a bottle of vintage 2008, after all it will be very special. It will have my footprints in it!

Hector Emanuelli 2012

To Tina

'Tis many moons now since we first met

midst those verdant hills

and sun kissed paths

of the valley of the Douro.

There you taught me

with such delight,

of the arts and custom of Portuguese life!

Then at last and out of the blue,

your telephone call to recall those happy days

I spent with you.

Of our whispered thoughts and secrets shared,

as we walked the paths of Miranda, Régua, Lanego,

and that happiest of days,

when we trod the grapes at Riva Lungo!

Then alas, our last evening meal,

across the table, your eyes met mine,

was that sadness I saw in your smile?

Your hand reached out, and finding mine,

we raised our glasses,

and toasted each other,

to life and love, with that

glorious Oporto Wine!

E. Emanuelli. 2009